505
ROCK 'N' ROLL
QUESTIONS

YOUR FRIENDS
CAN'T ANSWER

Other "505" books from Walker:

505 Baseball Questions Your Friends Can't Answer
   John Kingston
505 Football Questions Your Friends Can't Answer
   Harold Rosenthal
505 Hockey Questions Your Friends Can't Answer
   Frank Polnaszek

For Victor Chapin, whose idea this was

We would also like to thank Henry McNulty, Karen Rose, Nicholas Scarim, Sam Perkins, and Timothy Schaffner.

505
ROCK 'N' ROLL
QUESTIONS

YOUR FRIENDS
CAN'T ANSWER

Nicholas and
Elizabeth Schaffner

WALKER AND COMPANY / NEW YORK

Library of Congress Cataloging in Publication Data

Schaffner, Nicholas, 1953–
    505 rock 'n' roll questions your friends can't
answer.

    Includes index.
    1. Rock music—Miscellanea.   I. Schaffner,
Elizabeth.   II. Title.
ML3534.S3   784.5′4   80-54484
ISBN 0-8027-0674-6   AACR2
ISBN 0-8027-7171-8 (pbk.)

First published in the United States of America in 1981 by the Walker
Publishing Company, Inc.

Published simultaneously in Canada by John Wiley & Sons Canada, Limited,
Rexdale, Ontario.

ISBN: 0-8027-0674-6, cloth
      0-8027-7171-8, paperback

Library of Congress Catalog Card Number: 80-54484

Printed in the United States of America

10 9 8 7 6 5 4 3 2

Contents

Foreword

During the research and selection of our 505 Rock 'n' Roll Questions, we tried to keep two different criteria in mind. First, we wanted our questions to be challenging (though we did include some that even your friends might be able to answer; we don't want anyone to feel like a chump). But second—and equally important—we attempted to dream up questions (and answers) that might be interesting or entertaining in and of themselves, that might shed some light on some aspect of rock history and its legendary figures.

In other words, "Who played bass for Sam the Sham and the Pharaohs?"—or "What was the B-side of Elvis Presley's tenth Gold Record?"—just wouldn't do. Challenging perhaps, but hardly provocative. We're not out simply to stump you.

We hope readers will be able to share in some of the surprise, perplexity, merriment, and enlightenment that we ourselves experienced in compiling our 505 Rock 'n' Roll questions. Cheating is permitted; after all, *it's only rock 'n' roll–but we like it.*

Nicholas and Elizabeth Schaffner

Intro

Origins of Rock 'n' Roll
The Fifties
Elvis Presley

Origins of Rock 'n' Roll

1. Who is primarily responsible for giving the term "rock 'n' roll" its present meaning?

2. What was the first rock 'n' roll record to become widely popular?

3. What was the first rock 'n' roll record to make it into the national charts?

4. What was the first rock 'n' roll record to reach the Number One position in the national charts?

5. What was the original meaning of the term rock 'n' roll?

ANSWERS

1. *Alan Freed, who at the time was a disc jockey in Cleveland, is credited with popularizing the term rock 'n' roll. Freed had noticed the surge of interest young whites were showing toward Rhythm and Blues and he was looking for a term that would bypass any racial connotations. He found it with rock 'n' roll, which he claimed to have used for the first time in 1951.*

2. *There is no one correct answer to this question for it is the subject of raging debate among rock 'n' roll historians; however, here are some of the possible contenders: "The Fat Man," Fats Domino, 1949; "Rocket 88," Jackie Brenston, 1951; "Lawdy Miss Clawdy," Lloyd Price, 1952; "Crazy Man Crazy," Bill Haley and His Comets, 1953.*

3. *"Crazy Man Crazy" by Bill Haley and His Comets. In June of 1953, "Crazy Man Crazy" reached number 12 in the Billboard charts.*

4. *"Rock Around the Clock" by Bill Haley and His Comets. Originally released in 1954, the record initially saw little chart action. However, it was included in the soundtrack of the film, Blackboard Jungle, and upon the film's release "Rock Around the Clock" began to shoot up the charts. It reached the Number One position in the Billboard charts in July of 1955, and held that spot for eight weeks. "Rock Around the Clock" remains America's top selling rock 'n' roll single.*

5. *"Rock 'n' roll" was originally a black slang term for having sex.*

The Fifties

1. "Splish, Splash," recorded by Bobby Darin, has another distinction aside from being an enormous hit. What is it?

2. Which Buddy Holly song was inspired by John Wayne?

3. What was the original name of Bill Haley's Comets?

4. Chuck Berry holds a degree. In what field is it?

5. Which rock 'n' roll singer released instrumental tracks under the pseudonym of the Hawk?

6. What was Buddy Holly's first single?

7. On which Chuck Berry hits is Alan Freed credited as co-writer?

8. What song did Buddy Holly co-write with his mother?

9. Who were the only two major fifties rock 'n' roll artists who did *not* appear on the trend-setting television show, American Bandstand?

10. Buddy Holly launched the career of which major country artist?

11. What was the Million Dollar Quartet?

12. It is the established policy of American Bandstand that the performers mime along to their records, as opposed

to singing their songs live. Who is the only performer who did not comply with this rule?

13. Which singer/performer—who went on to become a top DJ on New York progressive radio in the late sixties and early seventies—had a hit with "Dinner With Drac" in 1958?

14. Which two pop singers were members of a local Philadelphia band called Rocco and The Saints?

15. What Chuck Berry song was originally titled "Ida Red" and where did Berry get the final name for the song?

16. How did Frankie Avalon achieve the vocal effect on his first hit, "De De Dinah"?

17. Who won the contest that Capitol Records ran in 1956 to discover a challenger to Elvis Presley?

18. Which rock 'n' roll innovator studied classical violin for seven years?

19. What was the original title for Little Richard's "Long Tall Sally"?

20. Where, when and why did Chuck Berry do his "duck walk" for the first time?

21. What song was the cause of Gene Vincent's receiving a conviction for "public lewdness and obscenity" from the Virginia State Court?

22. Carl Perkins was slated to be the first rock performer to appear on television, but it didn't work out that way. Why?

23. What song was Chuck Berry inspired to write after a tour of Australia?

24. Which Little Richard song was originally written as a stream of abuse directed at his boss in the diner of the Greyhound Bus Terminal in Macon, Georgia?

25. What was Bill Haley's first recording?

26. Who was Neil Sedaka's "Oh Carol" written for?

27. What song did Eddie Cochran's fiancée, Sharon Sheeley, write for Ricky Nelson?

28. What was Chuck Berry's first certified million seller?

29. "Party Doll" by Buddy Knox and "I'm Sticking With You" by Jimmy Bowen were actually recorded by one group but released under the names of the group's two vocalists. What was the name of the group?

30. The tragic airplane crash that took the life of Buddy Holly also killed two other rock stars. Who were they?

31. Which classic rock song was originally titled "Uncle John"?

32. Which vocalist had been a Golden Gloves boxing champion at the age of sixteen?

33. From the Drifters' initial formation in 1953 to the demise of the group in 1969, how many individual vocalists passed through their ranks?

34. What was the inspiration for "Blue Monday," a 1956 hit for Fats Domino?

35. What two firsts were accomplished by "Blue Suede Shoes," Carl Perkins's 1956 hit?

36. Who was Eddie Cochran's "Three Stars" a tribute to?

37. What was unusual about Marty Robbins's hit record, "El Paso," released in 1959?

38. Who are the two performers or groups—to become enormously influential and successful later on in their careers—who failed their auditions for Arthur Godfrey's Talent Scouts, a nationally broadcast television show designed to showcase promising amateur performers?

39. Who was the songwriter ("Lonely Teardrops," "Reet Petite") who in 1958 borrowed $700 to start his own record label?

40. What were the two records Buddy Holly produced for other artists?

ANSWERS

1. "Splish, Splash," released in 1958, was one of the first records to be recorded on an eight-track tape machine, an innovation which revolutionized recording possibilities.

2. "That'll Be the Day." Buddy Holly and Jerry Allison (drummer of the Crickets) were enthusiasts of the 1956 Western The Searchers, in which John Wayne starred. His catch phrase in the film was, "That'll be the day." Holly and Allison were so taken with the saying that they wrote a song around it.

3. The Saddlemen.

4. Cosmetology, from the Gibbs Beauty School.

5. Jerry Lee Lewis.

6. "Blue Days, Black Nights," released in April, 1956, on Decca Records.

7. "Maybellene" and "Nadine."

8. "Maybe Baby."

9. Elvis Presley and Ricky Nelson.

10. Waylon Jennings.

11. The Million Dollar Quartet was a jam session by Elvis Presley, Johnny Cash, Carl Perkins and Jerry Lee Lewis that took place at Sun Records in 1956. The session was recorded but none of it has ever been released.

12. Jerry Lee Lewis.

13. John Zacherle.

14. Frankie Avalon and Bobby Rydell.

15. *"Ida Red"* was the original title for *"Maybellene."* Contrary to popular opinion Berry did not get the name *"Maybellene"* from the cosmetic company of the same name. As he told Guitar Player Magazine in February 1971, *"She's a cow in a nursery rhyme that I ran across in third grade. I was thinking of a freaky name for a girl."*

16. He grew frustrated during the recording sessions and jokingly sang the song while pinching his nose closed with his fingers. His manager liked the effect and the song was recorded with Avalon singing in that way.

17. Gene Vincent.

18. Bo Diddley.

19. *"The Thang."*

20. Chuck Berry did his duck walk for the first time in 1956 at an Alan Freed Show at the Paramount Theatre in New York City. Enroute to the show Berry's suit became wrinkled and, as he said in a 1969 Rolling Stone interview: *"I actually did that duck walk to hide the wrinkles in the suit . . ."*

21. *"Woman Love,"* the flip side to his enormous hit *"Be-Bop-a-Lula."*

22. Carl Perkins was slated to appear on the Perry Como Show, but en route to the studio he was involved in a serious car accident in which he was hurt and, tragically, his brother was fatally injured.

23. *"Back in the U.S.A."* Berry told Rolling Stone in 1969, *"That was strictly my experience in Australia, which was a drag. I mean really a drag, I never found even a hot dog . . ."*

24. *"Tutti Frutti,"* Little Richard's first hit.

25. *"Rocket 88"* by Bill Haley and the Saddlemen, released by Essex Records in 1951.

26. *"Oh Carol"* was written for a young songwriter named Carole Klein, who later, in her incarnation as Carole King, became one of the top selling solo artists of the early seventies.

27. "Poor Little Fool."

28. "My Dingaling" in 1972.

29. The Rhythm Orchids.

30. Ritchie Valens and the Big Bopper.

31. "Bo Diddley" by Bo Diddley.

32. Jackie Wilson, who sang with the Drifters and with Billy Ward and the Dominoes and later enjoyed a successful career as a solo artist.

33. Thirty-two different vocalists.

34. The Blue Monday Club in New Orleans.

35. It was the first rockabilly Number One hit record and it was the first record to appear simultaneously in the Pop charts, the Country and Western charts and the Rhythm and Blues charts.

36. Buddy Holly, the Big Bopper and Ritchie Valens. Cochran himself was subsequently killed in a 1962 car crash.

37. At a running length of 5 minutes and 19 seconds, it was the longest song to have become a hit up to that time.

38. Elvis Presley and Buddy Holly and the Crickets. Elvis failed his audition in 1955. Buddy Holly and the Crickets failed theirs in 1957.

39. Berry Gordy, Jr., who started Motown Records, one of the recording industry's biggest success stories.

40. Buddy Holly produced "Jole Blon"/ "When Sin Stops" for Waylon Jennings in September of 1958. Later that year Holly produced "Stay Close To Me" / "Dontcha Know" for Lou Giordano. Holly played rhythm guitar on both of these singles.

Elvis Presley

1. When and where was Elvis Presley's first public appearance?

2. What was the first song Elvis Presley ever recorded?

3. What was the result when Elvis Presley went into Sun Records to record "I Love You Because" and several other country and western songs?

4. What was the first Presley record to appear on the national charts?

5. Who was Elvis Presley's first manager?

6. Where did the first riot over Presley occur?

7. What was the "unheard-of total" that RCA records paid Elvis Presley for signing with them in 1955?

8. What was Presley's first television appearance?

9. What was Presley's first Number One hit?

10. What was the "first" that Presley accomplished with the single, "Hound Dog"/"Don't Be Cruel"?

11. What was the Elvis Presley Midget Fan Club?

12. For which of Presley's singles was there such an enormous number of advance orders that RCA Records had to rent pressing plants from one of its competitors to

meet the demand?

13. What rank did Elvis Presley reach while overseas in the armed service?

14. What Elvis Presley hit is based on the classic Italian song "O Sole Mio"?

15. Where is Elvis Presley Park?

16. Presley was a member of which police departments?

17. Who were the "Memphis Mafia"?

18. Which one of Presley's hit singles remained in the charts for the longest time?

19. How many films did Presley star in?

20. Why did Elvis Presley request a meeting with President Nixon?

21. What was unusual about the 1970 Presley album, *On Stage*?

22. How many Presley singles appeared in the Pop charts during his lifetime?

23. Why did Elvis Presley volunteer to be an F.B.I. informant?

24. Why is there no street sign on Elvis Presley Boulevard in Memphis?

25. How many *certified* million-selling singles did Presley have, and what were their titles?

26. What was Elvis Presley's favorite kind of sandwich?

ANSWERS

1. *Elvis Presley's first public appearance took place when he was ten years old. He represented East Tupelo (his home town) in a talent competition at the Mississippi-Alabama Fair and Dairy Show. Presley, who sang "Old Shep" a cappella, won the second prize, which consisted of five dollars and a free pass to all the amusement rides.*

2. *The first songs Presley ever recorded were "My Happiness"/"That's When Your Heartaches Begin" as a birthday present for his mother. The recording was made at the Memphis Recording Service, an extension of Sun Records. It was a tape made of this rather inauspicious recording debut that brought Elvis to the attention of Sam Phillips, the owner of Sun Records.*

3. *During a session break Presley spontaneously burst into "That's All Right, Mama," a blues song by Arthur "Big Boy" Crudup, and the other musicians wholeheartedly joined in the fun, making what they thought was merely a terrific racket. Much to their surprise, Sam Phillips, who was producing the session, leapt into the room and said, "Hold it! That's just what I want." The song was duly recorded and released as Presley's first single.*

4. *"Baby, Let's Play House," Presley's fourth single, entered the national charts in July, 1955.*

5. *Bob Neal, a disc jockey on the Memphis radio station WMPS.*

6. *The first riot over Presley occurred in Jacksonville, Florida, in July of 1955. A mob of fans tore his clothing from his body and even removed his shoes for keepsakes.*

7. *RCA paid $40,000 to have Elvis Presley signed to their company. At that time, this was considered to be an enormous sum of money to a virtual unknown.*

8. *The Tommy and Jimmy Dorsey Stage Show in January, 1956.*

9. *"Heartbreak Hotel," released early in 1956.*

10. *With these two songs, Elvis Presley became the first artist simultaneously to hold the Number One and Number Two positions in the chart. What is even more impressive is that the two songs were the A-side and the B-side of the same single.*

11. *The Elvis Presley Midget Fan Club was one of many bizarre publicity stunts devised by Colonel Parker, Presley's manager. Parker, having a predilection for midgets, hired a large group of them, most of them Munchkins left over from the filming of the Wizard of Oz, to march through Hollywood proclaiming themselves the Elvis Presley Midget Fan Club.*

12. *"Love Me Tender."*

13. *In January 1960 Presley was promoted to the rank of Sergeant, commanding a three-man reconnaissance team for the Third Armored Division's 32nd Scout Platoon.*

14. *"It's Now or Never."*

15. *Elvis Presley Park is in his birthplace, Tupelo, Mississippi.*

16. *The Los Angeles Police Department, the Shelby County, Tennessee, Sheriff's Department, and the Memphis Police Department.*

17. *The "Memphis Mafia" were members of the circle of friends whom Presley surrounded himself with. They served as bodyguards and personal help to Presley.*

18. *"All Shook Up" remained at the Number One position for nine weeks and remained in the charts for a total of 30 weeks in 1957.*

19. *Presley starred in 33 films.*

20. *Presley wished to become a narcotics agent and he met with President Nixon to discuss the possibility of this.*

21. The record sleeve of On Stage doesn't have Presley's name on it anywhere. This was probably the first record ever made that omitted the artist's name on its cover.

22. 145.

23. According to an FBI memo, Presley felt that the Beatles and other groups were a bad influence on American youth and he wished to do something to counteract this.

24. Every time the town of Memphis has erected a street sign to mark Elvis Presley Boulevard it has been stolen by an overeager fan. The town board members have thrown up their hands in despair and the street now goes unmarked.

25. Presley had nine certified million sellers. They were: "Hard-headed Woman" (1958), "Can't Help Falling In Love" (1962), "In the Ghetto" (1969), "Suspicious Minds" (1969), "Don't Cry Daddy" (1970), "The Wonder of You" (1970), "Burning Love" (1972), "Way Down" (1977), and "My Way" (1977).

26. Peanut butter and bananas.

Hook

**The Beatles
The Rolling Stones
British Invasion**

The Beatles

1. How did the Beatles get their name?

2. What were the earliest recordings released by the Beatles?

3. What was the Beatles' first hit?

4. What instrument did John Lennon play on the Beatles' first three singles?

5. On what show did the Beatles first perform for U.S. television?

6. Where and when did the Beatles perform their first concert in the United States?

7. How many "legitimate" record labels have issued Beatles' product in the U.S.?

8. It is well-known that in 1968 the fabulous foursome launched their own label, Apple, with a Beatles single, "Hey Jude." What *other* (American) record company had previously been launched with a Beatles single?

9. What was the single that Capitol planned to release as its U.S. follow-up to "I Want To Hold Your Hand"—until Beatles' manager Brian Epstein persuaded the label not to?

10. What Beatles single, actually released and rising in the

Cash Box Top Hundred, was withdrawn from the market by Capitol at Epstein's request?

11. Which Beatles song has been recorded most often by other artists?

12. Which Beatles song did John, Paul, George, and Ringo all cite in early 1964 as their own favorite among the tracks they had released up to that time?

13. What was the first Lennon-McCartney song to become a Number One hit in the hands of another artist?

14. Who were the original artists to have hits with the following songs covered by the Beatles: "Baby It's You," "You've Really Got A Hold On Me," "Kansas City," "A Taste of Honey," and "Please, Mr. Postman"?

15. What was the reason for Capitol Records' release (virtually simultaneously in the summer of 1964) of three Beatles singles: "A Hard Day's Night"/"I Should Have Known Better," "I'll Cry Instead"/"I'm Happy Just To Dance With You," and "And I Love Her"/"If I Fell"?

16. What was the first Beatles' song to make no apparent reference whatsoever to "romance"?

17. On which Beatles song did Ringo Starr receive his first song-writing credit?

18. Which songs released by "the Beatles" were in fact solo efforts?

19. What was the largest audience the Beatles ever played to?

20. What did George Harrison consider the worst nightmare of the Beatles' career?

21. What was the first attempt by members of the Beatles to produce another artist's records?

22. Which Beatle visited America before the group was famous?

23. Which Beatles' song was the first to use reverse tapes?

24. How did George Harrison get interested in the sitar?

25. What college did two future Beatle wives attend?

26. Even those songs John and Paul composed separately were traditionally credited to "Lennon/McCartney." Which records finally broke with this tradition?

27. What Donovan hit was originally titled "Song For John and Paul"?

28. Match these names of the Beatles' songs, LPs and films with their original titles.

a. "Yesterday"   1. *That's A Nice Hat (Cap)*
b. Help!   2. *The Void*
c. "It's Only Love"   3. *Scrambled Egg*
d. "Tomorrow Never Knows"   4. *Get Back*
e. Revolver   5. *Beatle Bop*
f. "I've Just Seen A Face" 6. *Eight Arms to Hold You*
g. Let It Be   7. *I'm Backing the U.K.*
h. "Cry For A Shadow"   8. *Abracadabra*
i. "Sun King"   9. *Aunty Gin's Theme*
j. "Back In The U.S.S.R."   10. *Los Paranoias*

29. What Beatle song incorporated a refrain from "Frère Jacques"?

30. What was the first George Harrison song to be covered by a major group?

31. Which Beatle song introduced rock to the possibilities of feedback?

32. On April 4, 1964, the Beatles had the top five entries in *Billboard's* Hot Hundred Singles and were also Number One and Two in the album chart. What were the titles of these hit records?

33. What song did the Beatles record that had previously been a hit for anti-gay crusader Anita Bryant?

34. What was the difference between the British and the American versions of the LP, *Sgt. Pepper's Lonely Hearts Club Band*?

35. What and where is Strawberry Fields?

36. Who dreamed up the title *Sgt. Pepper's Lonely Hearts Club Band*?

37. Why did Paul McCartney select the age 64 for his song "When I'm 64"?

38. Which two Lennon/McCartney songs on *Sgt. Pepper* incorporated several lines contributed by an uncredited lyricist?

39. Which song on *Sgt. Pepper* made use of a melody Paul McCartney had composed in Liverpool as a teenager?

40. Where did the title for "Lucy In the Sky with Diamonds" come from?

41. What were the two titles originally announced for inclusion on *The Beatles* ("White Album"), and subsequently left off?

42. On which Beatles' song did John Lennon perform the vocal while lying on the floor to get the right vocal effect?

43. Many Beatle songs were inspired by some object or written work. Match the titles below with their inspirations.

a. *"Being For The Benefit of Mr. Kite"*
b. *"Savoy Truffle"*
c. *"Good Morning, Good Morning"*
d. *"The Inner Light"*
e. *"Tomorrow Never Knows"*
f. *"Golden Slumbers"*

1. *Breakfast cereal commercial*
2. *16-century poem by Thomas Dekker*
3. *Tibetan Book of the Dead*
4. *Victorian carnival poster*
5. *Box of Good News chocolates*
6. *Poem by Tao, the Chinese philosopher*

44. What Beatles' song did Frank Sinatra call "the greatest love song of the past 50 years"?

45. Which Beatle had three cats named Jesus, Joseph and Mary?

46. What were the "clues" that led many Beatles' fans to believe that Paul McCartney was dead?

47. What Beatles single featured Paul McCartney on drums and John Lennon on lead guitar because George Harrison and Ringo Starr were unavailable for the sessions?

48. Which Beatle used the pseudonym "L'Angelo Mysterioso"?

49. Which Beatles' song was banned from the British airwaves for "obscenity"?

50. What was the last record the Beatles ever made?

51. Which Beatle used the pseudonym "Dwarf Mac-Dougal"?

52. What was the Beatles' biggest selling single? Their biggest selling LP?

53. Not counting re-issues of old tracks, Apple/Capitol released 25 Beatles singles: "I Want To Hold Your Hand," "Can't Buy Me Love," "Hard Day's Night," "I'll Cry Instead," "And I Love Her," "Matchbox," "I Feel Fine," "Eight Days A Week," "Ticket To Ride," "Help!," "Yesterday," "We Can Work It Out," "Nowhere Man," "Paperback Writer," "Yellow Submarine," "Penny Lane," "All You Need Is Love," "Hello Goodbye," "Lady Madonna," "Hey Jude," "Get Back," "Ballad of John and Yoko," "Something," "Let It Be," and "The Long and Winding Road." Which *five* of the above fell short of attaining certification as million-selling Gold records?

54. Besides George Martin, what two well-known music industry figures produced a Beatles record?

55. Who is the only Beatle who has never been arrested for possession of marijuana?

56. Which of the Beatles used the pseudonym "Percy Thrillington"?

57. Who is the uncredited author of a few lines in John Lennon's song attacking Paul McCartney, "How Do You Sleep?"

58. What was the album for which George Harrison wrote his first liner notes?

59. What two Paul McCartney songs (one recorded by the Beatles, the other by Wings) share the same title?

60. Which two Beatles have written a song called "Woman"?

61. In 1970, Ringo Starr recorded three solo albums, each covering a specialized genre of music. The first was *Sentimental Journey* (pre-rock popular ballads); the second, *Beaucoups of Blues* (country and western songs). What was the third, never released, LP?

62. What is the only Beatle solo album to have hit Number One in its second week on the U.S. *Billboard* charts (as of this writing)?

63. Which Beatle described the group's break-up in a song that concluded with the wish that the Beatles get back together?

64. What Beatles song was selected in 1977 for inclusion on the Voyager Spacecraft recording (see question #4 in Odds and Ends), but (unfortunately, incredibly) was dropped on account of copyright complications?

65. What was the "worst" Beatles song ever?

66. Of all the Beatles' recordings, which ones by each member of the group were John Lennon's favorites?

67. In which of the Beatles' songs does the word "love" appear?

ANSWERS

1. *According to an article John Lennon wrote for* Mersey Beat *in July 1961: "It came in a vision—a man appeared on a flaming pie and said unto them 'from this day on you are Beatles with an A.'" More prosaically, in a 1964 interview John credited Buddy Holly and the Crickets (also a major musical influence) for inspiring the Beatles' name: "I was looking for a name like the Crickets that meant two things. From the Crickets I went to Beatles. When you said it, people thought of crawly things, when you read it, it was beat music."*

2. *In Hamburg in 1961 they were hired by Bert Kampfaert (composer of "Strangers in the Night") to back up British rock 'n' roll singer Tony Sheridan on six tracks, one of which, "My Bonnie," was released as a single (on which the group was billed as the Beat Brothers because Polydor Records thought "Beatles" would be too mystifying to the German audience). At these sessions the Beatles also recorded their own versions of "Ain't She Sweet" and a Lennon/Harrison instrumental titled "Cry for a Shadow." The first official recording by John, Paul, George, and Ringo was "Love Me Do" and "P.S. I Love You," issued by Parlophone in October 1962.*

3. *"Love Me Do" was a moderate hit in England, but their first Number One hit in that country was "Please Please Me." In America their first Number One hit was "I Want To Hold Your Hand."*

4. *Harmonica.*

5. *The Jack Parr Show, on January 3, 1964.*

6. *The Washington (D.C.) Coliseum, on February 11, 1964.*

7. *Ten. In chronological order: Vee-Jay, Swan, Capitol,*

MGM, Tollie, United Artists, Atco, Metro, Clarion, and Apple. One might include an eleventh label (chronologically the first), Decca, which had originally issued "My Bonnie" as by Tony Sheridan and the Beat Brothers—these last being, in fact, the Beatles.

8. Tollie. (The single was "Twist And Shout.")

9. "Roll Over Beethoven."

10. "Kansas City"/ "Boys."

11. "Yesterday."

12. "This Boy."

13. In Britain, "Do You Want To Know a Secret?" by Billy J. Kramer and the Dakotas (1963); in America, "World Without Love" by Peter and Gordon (1964).

14. "Baby It's You"—The Shirelles; "You've Really Got A Hold On Me"—The Miracles; "Kansas City"—Wilbert Harrison; "A Taste of Honey"—Martin Denny; "Please Mr. Postman"—Marvelettes.

15. Together with the previously released "Can't Buy Me Love," these songs comprised all but one of the Beatles' songs from the soundtrack LP, A Hard Day's Night, which the film's distributor, United Artists, was entitled to issue through its subsidiary record company. Capitol, however, had the right to exploit these recordings in any other format and so made the most of the opportunity. (Most of the songs were soon recycled yet a third time on the Capitol LP Something New.)

16. "Nowhere Man" (late 1965).

17. "What Goes On" (late 1965) was credited to "Lennon/McCartney/Starkey," though the last name was inadvertently omitted from the U.S. single.

18. Paul McCartney was on his own on: "Yesterday," "Why Don't We Do It in the Road," "Blackbird," "Mother Nature's Son," "Wild Honey Pie" and "Her Majesty." George Harrison soloed on:

"Love You Too," "Within You, Without You," and "The Inner Light." John Lennon was entirely responsible for "Revolution 9" and "Julia." Ringo Starr is the only Beatle heard on "Goodnight."

19. In 1965, the Beatles set a world record for the largest crowd ever gathered at a musical event. This was at Shea Stadium, in New York City, with 56,000 in attendance. The following year they broke that record at the Aranita Coliseum in Manila, the Philippines.

20. Being escorted out of the Philippines by furious mobs following the group's failure to attend a luncheon with President Marcos's wife. George said the Beatles first heard of the date when they saw their "snub" reported on the local TV news.

21. In mid-1965 Lennon and McCartney produced the Silkies' version of "You've Got to Hide Your Love Away."

22. George Harrison.

23. "Rain." "I just happened to have the tape on the wrong way 'round; it just came out backwards, it just blew me mind. The voice sounds like an old Indian."—John Lennon.

24. Through Ken Thorne's incidental music for Help!, which used a sitar on several tracks to get an "eastern" feel.

25. Sarah Lawrence, in Bronxville, N.Y. (Yoko Ono and Linda Eastman).

26. In 1967 the album of incidental music from the soundtrack of The Family Way was credited only to McCartney; then in 1969 the Plastic Ono Band single "Cold Turkey" was credited simply to "J. Lennon."

27. "Sunshine Superman."

28. a—3, b—6, c—1, d—2, e—8, f—9, g—4, h—5, i—10, j—7.

29. "Paperback Writer."

30. "If I Needed Someone" was covered by the Hollies. A controversy ensued when George called their version "rubbish"; the Hollies retaliated by blocking the single's release in the U.S.

31. *"I Feel Fine"; John Lennon claimed the searing introduction was produced by accident.*

32. *The singles were: "Can't Buy Me Love," "Twist And Shout," "She Loves You," "I Want to Hold Your Hand," and "Please, Please Me." The LPs were: Meet the Beatles and Introducing the Beatles.*

33. *"Till There Was You," which had been a hit for Anita Bryant in 1959.*

34. *The British version had a two-second sound collage in the run-out groove of side two, left off the U.S. edition.*

35. *Strawberry Fields is a Liverpool orphanage not far from Lennon's childhood home.*

36. *Mal Evans, the Beatles' late road manager.*

37. *Paul's father, Jim McCartney, had recently turned 64 at the time the song was recorded.*

38. *Both the title song and "Fixing a Hole" included lines by Mal Evans, who received a royalty but agreed that the "Lennon/McCartney" byline should remain intact.*

39. *"When I'm 64."*

40. *That was originally the title of a drawing by Julian Lennon, John's young son.*

41. *George Harrison's "Not Guilty" and John Lennon's "What's the News Mary Jane?"*

42. *"Revolution."*

43. *a—4, b—5, c—1, d—6, e—3, f—2.*

44. *"Something."*

45. *Paul McCartney.*

46. Vocal clues
"Strawberry Fields Forever": *John Lennon supposedly mut-*

ters "I buried Paul," at the end of the song. Actually he says "Cranberry sauce."

"Revolution 9": Played backwards, the chant of "number nine, number nine" is said to become "turn me on dead man, turn me on dead man." The song also contains sounds of a car crash, supposedly the way McCartney met his untimely demise.

"I'm So Tired"/"Blackbird": Played backwards, the gibberish between the tracks allegedly reveals the statement that "Paul is dead, man, miss him, miss him."

"A Day in the Life" and "Don't Pass Me By": Both songs are said to chronicle the entire story of the "fatal crash."

"I Am the Walrus": It was claimed that "walrus" is the Greek word for "corpse," and the track fades out with a reading from a death scene from Shakespeare's King Lear.

Visual clues
Abbey Road

- The cover purportedly shows the Beatles leaving a cemetery. John is dressed as a "minister," Ringo as an "undertaker," George as a "gravedigger," and Paul is out of step with the others.
- Paul is barefoot; it was said to be an English custom to bury their dead without shoes.
- Paul is holding a cigarette in his right hand; the "real" Paul was left-handed.
- The license plate of a nearby car reads "28 IF." Paul would have been 28 "if" he had lived. (Actually, he was only 27.)

Sgt. Pepper's Lonely Hearts Club Band

- There is a "grave" pictured on the cover, with yellow flowers on it arranged in the shape of Paul's bass guitar.
- A hand is extended over McCartney's head, an "omen of death," according to some.
- On the back cover, Paul is the only one of the Beatles

with his back to the camera.

Magical Mystery Tour

- On page 3 of the picture book that came with the record, Paul sits in front of a sign that says "I was" and two flags hang over his head as in a military funeral.
- On page 23, Paul's carnation is black, whereas the other Beatles wear red ones.

47. "The Ballad of John and Yoko."

48. George Harrison used that pseudonym while working as a session guitarist on Jack Bruce's Songs for a Tailor.

49. "I Am the Walrus"; the offending line was you let your knickers down.

50. "I Me Mine," recorded on January 3, 1970, which appeared on the last-issued album, Let It Be. However, the last album recorded in its entirety was Abbey Road, cut in the summer of 1969; the rest of Let It Be had been recorded in January, 1969.

51. John Lennon, for some Dylanesque acoustic strumming on Walls and Bridges. Dwarf was the name of Dylan's music publishing company and MacDougal was the name of the Greenwich Village street that Dylan lived on.

52. In America, "Hey Jude" and Abbey Road each sold 5 million copies within the first year of their release. In Britain, "She Loves You" and With the Beatles were the biggest sellers for the group.

53. "I'll Cry Instead," "And I Love Her," "Matchbox," "Ticket To Ride," and "The Long and Winding Road."

54. Bert Kampfaert ("Ain't She Sweet," "Cry For A Shadow," and six songs featuring Tony Sheridan, Hamburg, 1961); Phil Spector (Let It Be, 1970).

55. Ringo Starr.

56. Paul McCartney, for his own orchestral version of Ram.

57. *Allen Klein, manager of Lennon, Harrison, and Starr, who was a cause of McCartney's estrangement from the others. The line* since you're gone you're just another day *was one of Klein's contributions.*

58. Young Master of the Sarod, *by Ashish Khan, a North Indian classical musician.*

59. *"Hold Me Tight."*

60. *John Lennon and Paul McCartney; the former appears on 1980's* Double Fantasy; *the latter was written in 1966 for Peter and Gordon, under the pseudonym Bernard Webb. Paul wanted to know whether the song would sell without the use of his famous name.*

61. *An album of electronic music, concocted with a little help from Bee Gee Maurice Gibb.*

62. Living in the Material World, *by George Harrison.*

63. *Ringo Starr, whose "Early 70" (issued on the B-side of "It Don't Come Easy") included a description of his estranged colleagues, and ended with the line* when I go to town I want to see all three.

64. *"Here Comes the Sun."*

65. *In a WABC-FM radio poll conducted by Howard Smith of* The Village Voice *in 1971, the three top vote-getters in this category were "Revolution 9," "Mr. Moonlight," and "You Know My Name (Look Up the Number)."*

66. *According to his 1973 interview with* Melody Maker, *John Lennon's favorite Beatles recordings were: of his own songs—"Strawberry Fields Forever" and "I Am the Walrus"; by Paul—"Here There and Everywhere"; by George—"Within You, Without You"; by Ringo—"Honey Don't."*

67. *Of the 184 songs written and recorded by the Beatles, 77 include the word "love" in the lyric: "Love Me Do," "PS I Love You," "Please Please Me," "Ask Me Why," "Do You Want to Know* a Secret?," "I Saw Her Standing There," "There's a Place," "From Me to You," "Thank You Girl," "She Loves You," "I'll Get You," "Hold Me Tight," "I Wanna Be Your Man," "I Want to Hold Your Hand," "This Boy," "Can't Buy Me Love," "You Can't Do That," "Any Time at All," "And I Love Her," "I Should Have Known Better," "If I Fell," "I'm Happy Just to Dance with You," "Tell Me Why," "Things We Said Today," "When I Get Home," "I'll Be Back," "I Feel Fine," "She's a Woman," "Eight Days a Week," "I Don't Want to Spoil the Party," "I'll Follow the Sun," "I'm a Loser," "No Reply," "What You're Doing," "Another Girl," "I Need You," "The Night Before," "You've Got to Hide Your Love Away," "Yesterday," "It's Only Love," "We Can Work It Out," "Drive My Car," "If I Needed Someone," "Michelle," "I'm Looking Through You," "The Word," "For No One," "Here There and Everywhere," "Good Day Sunshine," "Love You Too," "Tomorrow Never Knows," "Sgt. Pepper's Lonely Hearts Club Band," "With a Little Help From My Friends," "Within You, Without You," "A Day in the Life," "All You Need Is Love," "Revolution," "Don't Pass Me By," "Helter Skelter," "Honey Pie," "I Will," "Julia," "Long Long Long," "Martha My Dear," "Revolution 1," "While My Guitar Gently Weeps," "Wild Honey Pie," "All Together Now," "It's All Too Much," "Don't Let Me Down," "Old Brown Shoe," "Because," "Her Majesty," "Something," "Across the Universe," "For You Blue," "Every Little Thing," "The End."

The Rolling Stones

1. What was the first Jagger/Richards composition ever recorded?

2. What was the first original composition the Stones recorded, and who was it credited to?

3. Who was the sixth member of the original Rolling Stones?

4. What was the first Jagger/Richards composition ever to register on the U.S. Top Hundred singles charts?

5. Most early Rolling Stones' press releases assigned them the following birthdates: Mick Jagger, July 26, 1944, Brian Jones, February 28, 1944, Charlie Watts, June 2, 1941, Keith Richards, December 18, 1944, and Bill Wyman, October 24, 1941. Only one of these is correct. Which?

6. What precedent was set by the Stones' first album (in Britain)?

7. Who was the MC who introduced the Stones to American television with such comments as "their hair is not that long, it's just smaller foreheads and higher eyebrows"?

8. Who were the two "uncles" in the title "Now I've Got a Witness (like Uncle Gene and Uncle Phil)" on the

Stones' first LP?

9. The Stones' first five British singles were: "Come On," "I Wanna Be Your Man," "Not Fade Away," "It's All Over Now," and "Little Red Rooster;" none was an original composition. Who were the rock singers or groups who first recorded them?

10. For a brief period in 1964, three consecutive Stones singles appeared simultaneously on *Billboard's* Hot Hundred. Which were they?

11. Which Rolling Stone listed his "interests" on 1964 questionnaires as "astronomy and cashew nuts"?

12. What were the first original compositions to appear on the A-side of a Rolling Stones single?

13. Which of the Rolling Stones' British Number One hits was never issued as a single in America?

14. Which Rolling Stones hit was re-recorded in Italian, for release as a single in Italy only?

15. Which Stones million seller was not originally intended for release as a single?

16. What was the first Rolling Stones album to consist entirely of Jagger/Richards compositions?

17. What two songs were recorded by both the Rolling Stones and the Beatles?

18. What was the notorious novel that inspired the mid-sixties stance of Mick Jagger, Keith Richards, and their manager, Andrew Loog Oldham—as well as the latter's liner notes for the Stones' albums?

19. Which Rolling Stones U.S. album track was in fact a studio run-through, substituted mistakenly by London Records for the finished version that appeared in Britain?

20. What was the Stones' first Number One album in America?

21. What was the title of Andrew Loog Oldham's documentary film about a Rolling Stones tour of Ireland?

22. Which Rolling Stone served in the Royal Air Force?

23. Why did the cover of *The Rolling Stones Now!* have to be reprinted?

24. What was the title of Charlie Watts's book?

25. What was the orchestral album produced by a Rolling Stone in 1966?

26. Which "picture sleeve" U.S. single depicted the Stones dressed and made up as women?

27. What was the title of the album that the Rolling Stones intended to release in 1966, but which their record company refused to issue under that name?

28. What was "Let's Spend Some Time Together"?

29. What was the first "solo" single by a Rolling Stone?

30. What was *Zoo of Flags*?

31. When Mick Jagger and Keith Richards were jailed in 1967 on drug charges, which other band immediately recorded two of their songs as a single to demonstrate their support? What were the songs?

32. How did the Rolling Stones get the title for *Between the Buttons?*

33. What Rolling Stones B-side, played by U.S. radio stations in lieu of the A-side, went on to become the Rolling Stones' second biggest hit up to that time?

34. Match the names of these Rolling Stones' albums to their originally announced titles:

a. *Metamorphosis*   1. *Tropical Diseases*
b. *The Rolling Stones*   2. *Sticky Fingers*
c. *Their Satanic*   3. *Have You Seen Your*
   Majesties Request   *Mother Live?*
d. *Let It Bleed*   4. *12 by 5*
e. *Got Live if You Want It* 5. *Cosmic Christmas*
f. *Exile on Main Street*   6. *Necrophilia*

35. Which Rolling Stones album cover is based on a line from a Bob Dylan song?

36. What two Rolling Stones singles featured Brian Jones on the Indian instruments, the sitar and the tambura?

37. What was the reason for the six-month delay in the release of the *Beggars Banquet* album?

38. In which countries were the following Stones' albums recorded: *Beggars Banquet, Goat's Head Soup,* and *Exile on Main Street?*

39. Match the rock performers to the songs the Rolling Stones bestowed upon them before finally recording them themselves.

a. "Sister Morphine"   1. Johnny Winter
b. "Wild Horses"   2. Chris Farlowe
c. "Silver Train"   3. Marianne Faithfull
d. "Think"   4. The Searchers
e. "Take It or Leave"   5. Gram Parsons

40. Which Rolling Stones song was completely banned by Chicago radio stations?

41. What were the Rolling Stones' five certified million-selling singles as of 1980?

42. Which two Rolling Stones LP covers were designed by Andy Warhol?

ANSWERS

1. "It Should Be You" recorded by George Bean on Decca Records, 1963.

2. "Stoned," an instrumental released in Britain in November, 1963, on the B-side of "I Wanna Be Your Man." It was credited to Nanker Phelge, a pseudonym used for songs composed by the entire group.

3. Pianist Ian Stewart, demoted to the status of road manager and behind-the-scenes accompanist by the Stones' manager, Andrew Loog Oldham, with the words: "He just doesn't look the part, and six is too many for them to remember the faces in the picture." (According to Keith Richards in a 1971 Rolling Stone interview.)

4. "That Girl Belongs To Yesterday," which the two Stones concocted for Gene Pitney. The single entered Billboard's Hot Hundred on January 18, 1964—a date which was highlighted by the debut appearance of the Beatles' first U.S. hit, "I Want to Hold Your Hand."

5. Charlie Watts. Jagger and Richards were each a year older than they would have you believe, Jones was two years older and Wyman, five!

6. The artists' names appeared nowhere on the front cover.

7. Dean Martin, on Hollywood Palace, June 5, 1964.

8. Gene Pitney and Phil Spector, both present at the sessions.

9. Chuck Berry, the Rolling Stones, Buddy Holly, the Valentinos, and Sam Cooke. (Note: John Lennon and Paul McCartney originally wrote "I Wanna Be Your Man" for the Stones: the Beatles only recorded it later. The very first recording of "Little Red

Rooster" was by Willie Dixon, the blues artist who wrote it.)

10. "Not Fade Away," "Tell Me," and "It's All Over Now."

11. Bill Wyman.

12. In America, "Tell Me;" in Britain, "The Last Time."

13. "Little Red Rooster."

14. "As Tears Go By" (as "Con Le Mie Lacrime").

15. "Satisfaction," the Rolling Stones' first U.S. Number One hit. Jagger told Melody Maker in 1965: "In Los Angeles we cut a lot of things and that was just one. We liked it, but didn't think of it as a single. Then London [Records] said they had to have a single immediately because we had a Shindig TV date and had to have something to plug. So they just released 'Satisfaction' as a single."

16. Aftermath, released in the spring of 1966.

17. "I Wanna Be Your Man" and "Money."

18. A Clockwork Orange, by Anthony Burgess.

19. "Everybody Needs Somebody to Love," on The Rolling Stones Now!

20. Out of Our Heads.

21. Charlie Is My Darling.

22. Bill Wyman.

23. Andrew Loog Oldham's liner notes contained the following "offensive" lines. "Cast deep into your pockets for loot to buy this disc of groovies and fancy words. If you don't have the bread, see that blind man, knock him on the head, steal his wallet and lo and behold you have the loot, if you put it in the boot, good, another one sold."

24. Ode to a High Flying Bird, a droll pictorial tribute to the late jazz innovator, Charlie "Bird" Parker.

25. *Keith Richards produced* Today's Pop Symphony *by the Aranbee Pop Orchestra.*

26. "Have You Seen Your Mother Baby Standing In the Shadow."

27. Could YOU Walk On the Water, *most of the contents of which surfaced as* Aftermath.

28. "Let's Spend Some Time Together" *was the version of* "Let's Spend The Night Together" *that the Stones cleaned up to perform on the Ed Sullivan Show.*

29. "In Another Land" *was issued in the U.S. in late 1967 as a solo single by Bill Wyman, though it subsequently appeared as a track on the Stones'* Their Satanic Majesties Request.

30. *The announced title of Charlie Watts's second picture book, a "bestiary" depicting each animal in terms of the flag of its country of origin. The book was never published.*

31. *The Who; the songs they recorded were "The Last Time" and "Under My Thumb."*

32. *Charlie Watts told* Melody Maker *in January 1967: "Andrew [Loog Oldham, the Stones' manager] told me to do the drawing for the album and he told me the title would go between the buttons [on the cover photo]. I thought he meant the title was 'Between the Buttons,' so it stayed. It was my fault because I misunderstood him."*

33. "Ruby Tuesday;" *the original A-side,* "Let's Spend The Night Together", *was widely banned because of its "suggestive content."*

34. *a—6, b—4, c—5, d—2, e—3, f—1.*

35. Get Your Ya-Ya's Out *depicts Charlie Watts and a mule that is wearing jewels and binoculars around its neck. Dylan's "Visions of Johanna" included the line: "The jewels and binoculars hang from the head of the mule."*

36. "Paint It Black" *and* "Street Fighting Man," *respectively.*

37. *Decca/London Records refused to distribute the original artwork, which depicted a lavatory wall covered with graffiti.*

38. *England, Jamaica, and France.*

39. *a—3, b—5, c—1, d—2, e—4.*

40. *In light of the riots that occurred at the 1968 Democratic convention, radio stations banned "Street Fighting Man," giving the excuse that they feared it would incite further violence.*

41. *"(I Can't Get No) Satisfaction," "Ruby Tuesday," "Honky Tonk Women," "Angie," and "Miss You."*

42. Sticky Fingers and Love You Live.

British Invasion

1. Who was the first British band, after the Beatles, to score an American Number One hit?

2. In 1963, what British band was cited by all four Beatles as being their favorite?

3. What was the song that producer George Martin wanted the Beatles to record as their second single and with which another group eventually had a Number One hit?

4. Who were the Beatmakers?

5. What did the Animals, Lulu, Donovan, Herman's Hermits and the Yardbirds have in common?

6. What major British Invasion-era group derived both its first two singles from Bob Dylan's debut LP?

7. Herman's Hermits, like many pop groups of the time, used session men on most of their recordings. On which three of their hits did they play every instrument themselves?

8. With what famous band did Mick Avory play drums before joining the Kinks?

9. What was the name of the group, heavily promoted in late 1964, whose key gimmick was the long, bleached

blond hair of all its members?

10. Which two bands released versions of the theme from *Batman* around the same time?

11. Which "heavy metal" pioneer's portfolio included a brief stint in Herman's Hermits?

12. What was the first major British band to tour behind the Iron Curtain?

13. Which guitarist can be heard on early hit records by the Who, the Kinks, Herman's Hermits, Donovan, Tom Jones, Cliff Richard, Brenda Lee, Marianne Faithfull, and many, many more?

14. Who was the Yardbirds' first lead guitarist?

15. Which British pop star married the fiancée of the late Eddie Cochran?

16. What did the Kinks and the Who have in common at the outset of their careers?

17. Match the performers with the films in which they appeared.

a. *The Ghost Goes Gear*	1. *The Zombies*
b. *The Swinging Set*	2. *Dave Clark Five*
c. *Bunny Lake Is Missing*	3. *The Yardbirds*
d. *Ferry Across the Mersey*	4. *Paul Jones (Manfred Mann)*
e. *Catch Us if You Can*	5. *Spencer Davis Group*
f. *Blow-up*	6. *Gerry and the Pacemakers*
g. *Privilege*	7. *The Animals*

18. Who was Donovan's "Jennifer Juniper"?

19. What mid-sixties group got sued by British Prime Minister Harold Wilson, and why?

20. What LP by a British group sold so poorly in the U.S. that its cover was turned into a jig-saw puzzle to promote the group's subsequent LP?

21. What Troggs song, considered to be in very poor taste, was banned in some countries and received only extremely restricted airplay in others?

22. What was the name of the song that the Who wrote and recorded for the American Cancer Society?

23. Which group took the Who's instrument-smashing routine a step further, to demolish cars and television sets on stage?

24. What instrument did Jimmy Page play during his first few months in the Yardbirds?

25. What are the only two studio recordings released by the Yardbirds that featured both Jimmy Page and Jeff Beck?

26. What were the original titles for the Who's *Tommy*?

27. Who flew from London to Los Angeles and straight back for the sole purpose of finishing songs, with the explanation, "I don't really like flying but I can't concentrate on the ground"?

28. What famous lead singer was nicknamed "Dippity Doo" by his fellow band members?

29. Who is the well-known bassist who studied cello at the Royal Scottish Academy of Music?

30. What was the Who's only Top Ten hit in the U.S.?

ANSWERS

1. Peter and Gordon. They had a Number One hit with "World Without Love" in June of 1964. The song was written for them by none other than Paul McCartney and John Lennon.

2. The Searchers.

3. "How Do You Do It" which was a British Number One hit for Gerry and the Pacemakers in the spring of 1963—and an American hit over a year later.

4. The Beatmakers was the name given to the group made up of members of the Beatles and Gerry and the Pacemakers. This band performed at the Litherland Town Hall in Liverpool before either of the two groups had begun their meteoric rise to fame.

5. They were all produced by Mickie Most.

6. The Animals. Undeterred by the failure of their version of "Baby Let Me Follow You Down," the Newcastle quintet went on to cover "House of the Rising Sun"—and hit the jackpot.

7. "Mrs. Brown You've Got a Lovely Daughter," "I'm into Something Good," and "Henry the VIII."

8. The Rolling Stones. Avory served as their drummer in 1962.

9. The Hullabaloos.

10. The Who and the Kinks. The Who on the "Ready, Steady, Who" EP and the Kinks on their album The Live Kinks.

11. Led Zeppelin's John Paul Jones toured Germany as the Hermits' organist, but, said Herman (Peter Noone), "He just didn't fit in."

12. Manfred Mann in October of 1965, followed a month later by the Animals.

13. *Jimmy Page.*

14. *Tony Topham, who was replaced by Eric Clapton, who was replaced by Jeff Beck, who was replaced by Jimmy Page.*

15. *Gordon Waller, of Peter and Gordon.*

16. *Along with having a four-man line-up and lasting talent, the Kinks and the Who shared a young American producer named Shel Talmy (who also made both bands record his ditty about a "Bald Headed Woman").*

17. *1—c, 2—e, 3—f, 4—g, 5—a, 6—d, 7—b.*

18. *Jennifer Boyd, George Harrison's sister-in-law, who ran a boutique called "Juniper."*

19. *The Move. To promote their 1968 single, "Flowers in the Rain," the group circulated postcards featuring a cartoon of Prime Minister Wilson in a compromising position with his secretary. Wilson sued them for all of the earnings made by "Flowers in the Rain." He won the suit and donated the proceeds to charity.*

20. Village Green Preservation Society, *released by the Kinks in 1968.*

21. *"I Can't Control Myself," the offending line being* your slacks are low and your hips are showing.

22. *"Little Billy." The song, which tells the story of an obese non-smoker who ends up raising all of his friends' children after their nicotine-addicted parents had died of lung cancer, was intended for radio airplay in an attempt to discourage young people from smoking tobacco. Unfortunately, it never made it onto the airwaves in the manner that was originally intended, although it did surface years later on the LP* Odds and Sods.

23. *The Move.*

24. *When bassist Paul Samwell-Smith angrily left the Yardbirds in 1966 they needed a replacement in a hurry, for they had contractual obligations to fulfill. The members of the band cajoled Jimmy Page into joining as a bass player, even though* he'd never played bass before. He served in this capacity for several months until Chris Dreja, who previously had played rhythm guitar, became competent enough on bass to take over.

25. "Happenings Ten Years' Time Ago," and "Psycho Daisies," released in October, 1966.

26. Amazing Journey, Deaf, Dumb and Blind Boy and Journey Into Space. Peter Townshend was especially taken with the last title, but was prevented from using it because there had previously been a radio show of the same name.

27. Ray Davies.

28. Roger Daltrey. He acquired the nickname as a result of his frequent use of the hair care product of the same name.

29. Jack Bruce.

30. "I Can See for Miles," which entered the Top Ten of Billboard's Hot Hundred in November, 1967.

Verse

Bob Dylan

Pop, Folk and Psychedelia

Bob Dylan

1. How much did Dylan's first album cost Columbia to record?

2. What was Dylan's first rock 'n' roll single?

3. Why did Bob Dylan order Phil Ochs out of his car in the middle of nowhere?

4. Which Dylan song was an almost note-for-note parody of a Beatles song?

5. According to Dylan, who did the best cover versions of his songs?

6. What Dylan single was issued only in Europe?

7. What was Bob Dylan's first Gold record?

8. What unusual feature was shared by the following Dylan compositions, all hit singles for Dylan or another artist: "Subterranean Homesick Blues," "Positively 4th Street," "Rainy Day Women #12 and #35," "Wigwam," "My Back Pages," "Just like Tom Thumb's Blues," and "She Belongs to Me"?

9. Which among Dylan's string of mid-sixties "electric" singles featured the services of the Band?

10. What was the official explanation for the title "Rainy

Day Women #12 and #35" (a.k.a. "Everybody Must Get Stoned")?

11. From which Dylan song did the notorious late sixties radical group, the Weathermen, derive its name?

12. Apart from "greatest hits" packages, which two Dylan albums have sold over a million copies in America (as of 1980)?

13. For which bestselling album (apart from his own *Self Portrait* and *Planet Waves*) did Dylan do the cover artwork?

14. What object did Dylan carry about with him on a 1965 tour?

15. What Dylan number has been released under two different titles that, together, comprise the key phrase in the song's chorus?

16. What was the name of the character played by Bob Dylan in the film *Pat Garrett and Billy the Kid*?

17. What was Dylan's first Number One album (in America)?

18. What convention was shattered by Dylan's single "Like a Rolling Stone"?

19. What song was Dylan prohibited by the CBS television network from performing on the Ed Sullivan Show?

20. What Dylan song did Jimmy Carter quote in his acceptance speech at the 1976 Democratic National Convention?

21. Which three Beatles attended Dylan's 1969 concert at the Isle of Wight?

22. What phrase from an earlier Dylan song was the originally announced title of Dylan's 1974 LP, *Planet Waves?*

23. With which recording star did Dylan re-record "Buckets of Rain" as a duet?

24. What Dylan album was planned as a collaboration with the Byrds?

25. What is the title of D. A. Pennebaker's seldom-seen surrealistic documentary of Dylan's 1966 European tour?

26. What multi-million dollar enterprise derived its name from a Bob Dylan song?

27. When and where was Dylan's first major performance with an electric rock band—and what was the name of the band?

28. Name five people who shared songwriting credits with Bob Dylan.

29. Which of the following did *not* record a Dylan song: Olivia Newton-John, Elvis Presley, the Grateful Dead, George Harrison, Johnny Cash, the Hollies, Van Morrison, the Animals, Jimi Hendrix, Richie Havens, Cher, Tom Robinson, the Flamin' Groovies, Donovan?

30. When Dylan briefly left Columbia for Asylum Records, what was the single that Columbia released in response?

ANSWERS

1. $402.

2. "Mixed Up Confusion," released in 1962 but quickly withdrawn from circulation. His first rock 'n' roll hit was "Subterranean Homesick Blues" in early '65.

3. Dylan was irked because Phil Ochs had said that "Can You Please Crawl out Your Window?", Dylan's follow-up single to "Like a Rolling Stone" and "Positively 4th Street," would flop. It did.

4. "Fourth Time Around" from Blonde on Blonde parodied "Norwegian Wood." John Lennon said it made him "very paranoid."

5. Manfred Mann.

6. "If You've Gotta Go, Go Now."

7. Bringing It All Back Home, in 1965.

8. In no case is the title (normally an important "hook") heard in the actual song.

9. "Can You Please Crawl Out Your Window?" and "One of Us Must Know."

10. A woman and her daughter came into the studio out of the rain during the recording sessions; upon ascertaining their ages, Dylan allegedly christened the song in their honor.

11. "Subterranean Homesick Blues" (you don't need a weatherman to know which way the wind blows).

12. Nashville Skyline and Desire.

13. Music from Big Pink, by the Band.

14. *A giant light bulb.*

15. *"Stuck Inside of Mobile with the," "Memphis Blues Again."*

16. *Alias.*

17. Planet Waves.

18. *The six-minute running length was two to three times that then thought acceptable to Top Forty radio programmers. Even so, "Like a Rolling Stone" became a Number One hit.*

19. *"Talkin' John Birch Society Blues." It was thought that this tale of Red baiting and paranoia would offend members of the distinguished Society. (The selection was also deleted from the album* The Freewheelin' Bob Dylan.)

20. *"It's All Right Ma (I'm Only Bleeding)." The line Carter quoted was* he who is not busy being born is busy dying.

21. John Lennon, George Harrison, and Ringo Starr.

22. Ceremonies of the Horsemen (from "Love Minus Zero").

23. Bette Midler.

24. Self Portrait.

25. Eat that Document.

26. Rolling Stone *magazine, from the song "Like a Rolling Stone."*

27. *July 25, 1965, at Rhode Island's Newport Folk Festival—where Dylan was roundly booed for the outrage; his accompanists were the Paul Butterfield Blues Band.*

28. *Rick Danko ("This Wheel's on Fire")*
Richard Manuel ("Tears of Rage")
George Harrison ("I'd Have You Anytime")
Jacques Levy (most of the Desire LP)
Tim Drummond ("Saved")
Dylan also collaborated with Allen Ginsberg on an album that has never been released.

29. *Donovan.*

30. *"A Fool Such as I," Dylan's rendition of the 1959 Elvis Presley hit.*

Pop, Folk and Psychedelia

1. Which international hit record was based on a traditional African folk song?

2. Though their early music was in celebration of the surf and those who ride it, only one of the Beach Boys was actually a surfer. Which one?

3. What are the seven different names under which the Four Seasons have recorded?

4. When Brian Wilson ceased performing in concerts with the Beach Boys in 1964, who was his original replacement?

5. What 1965 Top Ten hit was based on the "Minuet in G" by Bach?

6. What was the name of the only solo record Brian Wilson ever released?

7. Which Beach Boys' Top Ten hit record was released against the groups wishes?

8. What was the Beach Boys' only certified million-selling single?

9. Who was the "first tycoon of teen"?

10. Which musician—later to become tremendously influ-

ential and successful—auditioned unsuccessfully for the Monkees?

11. Who wrote the Monkees' hit "I'm a Believer"?

12. What was the first song from the emerging West Coast "counterculture" to become a Top Ten hit?

13. What was the first "counterculture" song to become a Number One hit?

14. Who was Jimmy James, of Jimmy James and the Blue Flames?

15. The vocal of "Barbara Ann," the Beach Boys' hit, is a duet between Brian Wilson and another singer. Who is the other singer?

16. What precipitated Phil Spector's "retirement" from the music industry?

17. What San Francisco "underground" band's first Columbia record release consisted of five simultaneously released singles?

18. Which famed guitarist was a paratrooper in the 101st Airborne Division of the U.S. Air Force?

19. Where did Pink Floyd get the title for their first LP, *Piper At the Gates of Dawn?*

20. Who was the first female lead singer in the Jefferson Airplane?

21. Which rock singer starred in the 1967 film, *War?*

22. What was *Smile?*

23. Which singer was voted "Ugliest Man on Campus" at

the University of Texas?

24. Which group recorded the first rock 'n' roll religious mass?

25. The leader of which group referred to himself and his band as "erotic politicians"?

26. Which rock album had liner notes written by the late Senator Hubert Humphrey?

27. Who were the rock and soul artists that Jimi Hendrix backed up before becoming famous in his own right?

28. What songs did Vice-President Spiro Agnew cite as being unfit for radio play because of supposed drug references in their lyrics?

29. Which album, released in 1968, is dedicated to Beat poet and personality, Neal Cassady?

30. Which Doors song contains in its lyrics two lines from a William Blake poem?

31. What song was largely responsible for the short-lived late sixties fad of smoking dried banana peels?

32. Which band did the Monkees expressly request as their supporting act on their 1967 summer tour?

33. Who produced the second Buffalo Springfield album, *Buffalo Springfield Again?*

34. How long did it take the Cream to record their second album, *Disraeli Gears?*

35. Which Jefferson Airplane song is a tribute to writer James Joyce?

36. In 1968, which pop star opened a boutique in Greenwich Village called "Zilch I"?

37. Why was a full-page ad taken in the Los Angeles *Free Press* telling people *not* to buy Lovin' Spoonful records and *not* to attend their concerts?

38. What was the original title for the Jefferson Airplane's album, *After Bathing at Baxter's?*

39. Which singer/songwriter wrote three songs for the 1968 Broadway play, *Jimmy Shine*, which starred Dustin Hoffman?

40. What five groups rose out of the rubble of Buffalo Springfield?

41. What is the hit song that Michael Nesmith of the Monkees wrote for Linda Ronstadt?

42. Which Beach Boys song was co-written with the mass murderer, Charles Manson?

43. Which rock group was responsible for organizing the Monterey Pop Festival?

44. What Doors' album got its title from a song that was left off the record, and that later turned up on a different LP?

45. Where did Crosby, Stills, Nash and Young make their debut performance?

46. What was the only part of the Doors' epic cycle of poetry and song, "The Celebration of the Lizard," to be released as a *studio* segment?

47. Who were the guitarist and the "revolutionary" who became embroiled in an onstage dispute at Woodstock?

48. Which famed groups originally went under these names: a) the Warlocks b) Levon and the Hawks c) the Beefeaters d) the Golliwogs?

49. What was the original title for Van Morrison's "Brown Eyed Girl"?

50. What are the names of the two films that Jim Morrison of the Doors co-directed with Paul Ferrara and Frank Lisciandro?

ANSWERS

1. "The Lion Sleeps Tonight" by the Tokens, a Number One hit in December of 1961.

2. Dennis Wilson.

3. The Four Lovers (1956), Frankie Valli and the Romans (1959), Billy Dixon and the Topics (1960), Hal Miller and the Rays (1961), Frankie Valli and the Four Seasons (1963), Larry and the Legends (1964), and Wonder Who (1966).

4. Glen Campbell.

5. "Lover's Concerto" by the Toys, a Top Ten hit in October of 1965.

6. "Caroline, No"/"Summer Means New Love." The single was released in 1966.

7. "Barbara Ann." Capitol Records released this single without the group's knowledge. It is unlikely that the Beach Boys begrudged the earnings they made with this successful single, but at a time when they were attempting to become more progressive, the simplistic silliness of "Barbara Ann" hardly gave them the musical credibility they desired.

8. "Good Vibrations."

9. Phil Spector, by far the most innovative record producer of the early 60's. His credits include production on the Ronettes' "Be My Baby," "Walking in the Rain," and "Baby I Love You;" the Crystals' "Then He Kissed Me," "He's a Rebel," and "Da Doo Ron Ron;" and Ike and Tina Turner's "River Deep, Mountain High." Almost every record he touched turned to Gold and Spector was a millionaire before he reached the age of twenty-five.

10. Stephen Stills (of Crosby, Stills, Nash and Young).

11. *Neil Diamond.*

12. "Somebody to Love," by the Jefferson Airplane, reached Number Five in Billboard's Hot Hundred in June of 1967.

13. "Light My Fire," by the Doors, reached Number One in Billboard in July, 1967.

14. *Jimi Hendrix.* Jimmy James and the Blue Flames was the name of the band Hendrix formed in 1966. It was while playing with this group in small New York City clubs that he was discovered by his eventual manager, Chas Chandler (ex-Animal), who took him to England, changed his name and his image, and the rest, as they say, is history.

15. *Dean Torrence, of Jan and Dean.*

16. Spector was justifiably miffed when the single he had produced for Ike and Tina Turner, "River Deep, Mountain High," only reached #88 in Billboard's Hot Hundred. He retired in a huff, but overcame his pique by 1969, when he resumed work as a producer.

17. *Moby Grape.*

18. *Jimi Hendrix.*

19. "Piper at the Gates of Dawn" was a chapter heading in Kenneth Grahame's children's novel, Wind in the Willows.

20. Signe Toly Anderson, who left the group when she became pregnant.

21. *Eric Burdon.* The film, made in England, was not a great success and could not find a distributor in the United States.

22. Smile was the name of a never-released Beach Boys album. The brain-child of Brian Wilson, Smile was loudly lauded by the privileged few who heard it as an absolute masterpiece. Its release was greatly anticipated, but early in 1967, Brian Wilson, feeling that there was a mystical connection between the recording sessions of the album's track "Fire" and an outbreak of small brush fires in Southern California, totally abandoned the project (though a few of the less adventurous tracks have surfaced on subsequent LPs).

23. Janis Joplin. Justifiably devastated by this cruelty, Janis fled to the more hospitable climate of San Francisco.

24. The Electric Prunes. They released their Mass in F Minor in 1968. To boost the authenticity of the record, the lyrics were in Latin. However, the quality of the music was beyond help.

25. Jim Morrison of the Doors.

26. Crimson and Clover by Tommy James.

27. Jimi Hendrix was one of James Brown's Famous Flames; he also backed up Little Richard, Joey Dee and the Starlighters, the Isley Brothers, Wilson Pickett, B. B. King, Ike and Tina Turner, Jackie Wilson and Curtis Knight and the Squires.

28. "Magic Carpet Ride" by Steppenwolf, "With a Little Help from My Friends" and "Lucy in the Sky with Diamonds" by the Beatles, "Acid Queen" by the Who, "Eight Miles High" by the Byrds, and "White Rabbit" by the Jefferson Airplane.

29. Anthem to the Sun by the Grateful Dead.

30. "End of the Night," which is on the first Doors album, titled simply The Doors.

31. "Mellow Yellow" by Donovan.

32. The Jimi Hendrix Experience. Hendrix's flamboyantly sexual stage act proved to be too much for young Monkees' fans to take and halfway through the tour the Jimi Hendrix Experience was dropped from the show.

33. Jim Messina. He later joined the group as replacement for bassist Bruce Palmer.

34. Four days. Eric Clapton described the sessions as being a *"sort of impromptu thing."*

35. *"Rejoyce."* Originally titled *"Ulysses,"* it contains lines from the novel of the same name by James Joyce.

36. David Jones of the Monkees.

37. There was a movement among the "underground" to blacklist the Lovin' Spoonful owing to the involvement of band members Zal Yanovsky and Steve Boone in a set-up drug bust. Sadly, the unpleasantness surrounding this incident contributed to the break-up of the Spoonful shortly thereafter.

38. Good S**t. RCA Records adamantly refused to release the album under that title.

39. John Sebastian.

40. Crosby, Stills, Nash and Young; Manassas; Poco; Loggins and Messina; Souther, Hillman and Furay.

41. *"Different Drum."*

42. *"Never Learn not to Love,"* which is included on the 20/20 LP. Manson does not receive a credit on the record. The same song with a different title appears on Manson's solo album.

43. The Mamas and Papas, principally John and Michelle Phillips from the group.

44. Waiting for the Sun.

45. At Woodstock.

46. *"Not to Touch the Earth,"* which appears on the *Waiting for the Sun* LP.

47. Peter Townshend was the guitarist and Abbie Hoffman was the "revolutionary." Hoffman leapt onstage during the Who's set at Woodstock to deliver a political harangue, Townshend quite neatly knocked him back into the audience.

48. a) the Grateful Dead b) the Band c) the Byrds d) Creedence Clearwater Revival.

49. *"Brown Skinned Girl."* Morrison *changed the title, feeling that radio stations would ban a song about a "mixed" relationship. However, many stations banned it anyway, finding the line* making love on the grass behind the stadium *offensive.*

50. Feast of Friends *and* HiWay.

Chorus

The Seventies
New Wave

The Seventies

1. What rock band was asked in 1970 to compose a ballet that was to feature Rudolf Nureyev?

2. What was Elton John's recording debut?

3. What is the name of the recording studio that Jimi Hendrix built?

4. What was the recording debut of Robert Plant, Led Zeppelin's lead singer?

5. Which major artist formed a group called Hype after enjoying his first big hit?

6. Which rock performer's mother played Saffire on the Amos 'n Andy TV show?

7. What 1970 hit single by the Guess Who was banned by several southern states because it was thought to be "communistic"?

8. Which singer/songwriter got his start backing up Warhol star Nico in the sixties?

9. In place of which band—to become enormously successful in the late seventies—was a group of imposters sent on a major U.S. tour by the genuine group's estranged manager?

10. When Led Zeppelin were forming, which lead singer

did they originally want for the band?

11. What was the first film that David Bowie appeared in?

12. What 1973 hit song was written about a fire that destroyed the Montreux Casino in Switzerland?

13. Prior to the formation of the Allman Brothers band, Duane Allman served as a session guitarist for which performers?

14. On their first European tour, what name were Led Zeppelin booked under?

15. Lynyrd Skynyrd's 1974 hit single, "Sweet Home Alabama," was an angry rebuttal to what other rock song?

16. From their formation in 1967 to the present, how many changes in personnel have Fleetwood Mac undergone?

17. What is the only Bruce Springsteen song to have become a Number One hit?

18. Which rock star was briefly a teacher at P.S. 75 in New York City?

19. Which successful British band has never had a permanent bassist in their line-up?

20. Which rock star won the National Squirrel Shooting Archery Contest in 1974?

21. In August of 1971, Linda Ronstadt's backing musicians decided to form a band and step out on their own. What is the name of this band?

22. Why did Led Zeppelin book themselves as the Nobs when they played in Denmark in 1970?

23. What rock star used a chest X-ray of a heart disease patient on the cover of his first album?

24. Which two recording artists were former recording engineers for the Beatles?

25. What was the first commercial release that Gregg and Duane Allman played on?

26. Which top selling single was based on Rachmaninoff's Third Piano Concerto?

27. Who was the first band to sign to Casablanca Records?

28. Which artist or group appeared simultaneously on the covers of *Time* and *Newsweek* magazines in 1975?

29. What Led Zeppelin hit was released as a single against the group's wishes?

30. What band was formed as the result of an ad in *Rolling Stone* magazine that read "Drummer willing to do anything to make it"?

31. What hit song was Lou Leiberman inspired to write after seeing Don McLean in concert?

32. What popular rock duo is made up of two refugees from the fifties instrumental group, the Champs?

33. Which rock star was married onstage at Madison Square Garden?

34. In 1975 Elton John and John Lennon each sang backing vocals on the other's single. What were those two singles?

35. Which band had as part of their stage set the lightning machine that had been designed and built for the original movie of *Frankenstein*?

36. Which Led Zeppelin song is dedicated to Joni Mitchell?

37. Bob Seger and the Silver Bullet Band originally went under what name?

38. Which one of David Bowie's hit singles was written with John Lennon?

39. From February 25 to March 4, 1978, the Bee Gees held the top three positions in the U.S. singles charts. What were these three songs?

40. Which Anglo-American band contained musicians who at one time were members of King Crimson, Spooky Tooth, and the Hunter-Ronson band?

41. The middle section of David Bowie's "Move On" (from the *Lodger* LP) is actually note for note another Bowie song played backwards. What is the other song?

42. Where did Fleetwood Mac get the titles for the following albums: *Mystery to Me*, *Penguin* and *Tusk*?

43. Who originally recorded "Air that I Breathe," the song that was a huge hit for the Hollies in 1974?

44. Who played piano on the Hollies hit "He Ain't Heavy, He's My Brother"?

45. Which hit song of the seventies was a tribute to Buddy Holly?

ANSWERS

1. *Pink Floyd. The project, however, ultimately fell through.*

2. *Elton John made his recording debut in 1965, singing "Come Back Baby" with the group, Bluesology.*

3. *Electric Ladyland. The studio, built to Hendrix's specifications, was completed shortly before his death in 1971. Electric Ladyland is still functioning, however, and is considered to be one of the best recording studios in the U.S.*

4. *Plant made his recording debut on an album by veteran British bluesman Alexis Korner called* Bootleg Him. *Plant sings lead vocal on the track "Operator."*

5. *David Bowie, early in 1970 following the success of "Space Oddity." Hype featured Mick Ronson on guitar, Tony Visconti on bass, and John Cambridge on drums. They played several gigs but never released a record.*

6. *Billy Preston's mother played Saffire.*

7. *"Share the Land."*

8. *Jackson Browne.*

9. *Fleetwood Mac. The real Fleetwood Mac eventually brought legal action to bear on the fraudulent Fleetwood Mac, but, unfortunately, not before many fans were ripped off by this sham.*

10. *Terry Reid, who was not available, having prior commitments at the time, but who recommended a young newcomer named Robert Plant.*

11. Virgin Soldiers.

12. *"Smoke on the Water."*

13. *Duane Allman worked sessions with Aretha Franklin, Delaney and Bonnie, King Curtis, Boz Scaggs, Ronnie Hawkins and Eric Clapton (most notably the classic* Layla *album).*

14. *The New Yardbirds.*

15. *"Southern Man" by Neil Young.*

16. *Ten.*

17. *"Blinded by the Light," written by Bruce Springsteen, but performed by the Manfred Mann Earthband. The song reached Number One in February, 1977.*

18. *Gene Simmons of Kiss. He taught for six months but quit because he "couldn't stand the kids."*

19. *Roxy Music.*

20. *Ted Nugent.*

21. *The Eagles. Since the formation of the band in 1971, the line-up has changed and now the only two band members who backed up Ronstadt are Glenn Frey and Don Henley.*

22. *When Led Zeppelin arrived in Denmark in 1970, quite a fuss was was being raised by Ms. Eva von Zeppelin, a relative of the designer of the airship and a resident of Copenhagen. She threatened lawsuits if the band performed under the Zeppelin name, telling the press, "They may be world famous, but a couple of shrieking monkeys are not going to use a privileged family name without permission." The group obligingly changed their name for the Copenhagen concert.*

23. *This somewhat grisly photo appeared on the cover of John Entwistle's first solo album,* Smash Your Head Against the Wall.

24. Hurricane Smith ("Oh Babe What Would You Say") and Alan Parsons (I Robot, Pyramid, etc.).

25. "Spoonful," a cover of the Willie Dixon song. The single was released under the name of the Allman Joys in 1965.

26. "All by Myself," a hit for Eric Carmen in March of 1976.

27. Kiss.

28. Bruce Springsteen.

29. "Whole Lotta Love." Atlantic Records attempted to comply with the group's wish that the track not be released as a single. However, when radio stations took it upon themselves to edit the song (its five-minute, 35-second running time was considered too long for Top Forty stations), Atlantic felt pressured into releasing an "authentic" version. It became one of Led Zeppelin's all-time biggest hits.

30. Kiss.

31. "Killing Me Softly with His Song," which was a Number One hit for Roberta Flack in 1973.

32. Seals and Crofts.

33. Sly Stone, in 1974.

34. John Lennon sang backing vocals on Elton John's cover version of "Lucy in the Sky with Diamonds," and Elton John sang and played on Lennon's "Whatever Gets You Through the Night."

35. Kiss.

36. "Going to California," on Led Zeppelin's fourth album.

37. The Bob Seger System.

38. *"Fame."*

39. *1. "Stayin' Alive" 2. "How Deep Is Your Love" 3. "Night Fever."*

40. *Foreigner.*

41. *"All the Young Dudes."*

42. Mystery to Me. *Mystery to me is a line from the album's opening track, "Emerald Eyes." Penguin. Fleetwood Mac's logo was a penguin. Tusk. Tusk is drummer Mick Fleetwood's pet name for a certain part of his anatomy.*

43. *Phil Everly.*

44. *Elton John. It was his first bona fide job as a session musician.*

45. *"American Pie," by Don McLean, which was a Number One hit for four weeks in 1972.*

New Wave

1. The Rich Kids, the Professionals, the Spectres and Public Image Limited all sprang from the ruins of which notorious band?

2. Which well-known singer is featured on the 1968 LP, *Wind in the Willows*, by a folk rock band of the same name?

3. The nucleus of which band had the following names before settling on their present one: the Phone; the Mirrors; the Outsiders; the Psychotic Negatives; the Weak Heartdrops?

4. What was the name of Elvis Costello's bluegrass group?

5. The Cars, the Talking Heads and the Necessaries all contain refugees from which innovative mid-seventies band?

6. When CBS Records released the Clash song, "Remote Control," as a single, against the group's wishes, what song did Strummer-Jones write in retaliation?

7. What was the name of the group that backed up Elvis Costello on his first LP, *My Aim Is True*?

8. Which new wave musician served a stint with Eric Burdon and the Animals in the late sixties?

9. Which lead singer wrote criticism for the English music paper, *New Musical Express*, prior to becoming well known?

10. The father of which new wave singer was voted tenth best singer in the 1961 *Melody Maker's* Reader's Poll?

11. What song by the Tom Robinson Band was written for Ray Davies of the Kinks?

12. Which Ramones song did Phil Spector work on prior to producing their album, *End of the Century*?

13. Which British performer was a lecturer at art colleges before becoming a rock 'n' roller?

14. Which new wave musician co-wrote "Show Me the Way," the song that was a massive hit for Peter Frampton in 1976?

15. Match these performers or groups to the films in which they appeared:

    a. B-52's   1. *Rude Boy*
    b. The Clash   2. *Rock 'n' Roll High School*
    c. Elvis Costello   3. *Quadrophenia*
    d. The Ramones   4. *Americathon*
    e. The Sex Pistols   5. *Ride a Rock Horse*
    f. Debbie Harry   6. *The Great Rock 'n' Roll
       (Blondie)   Swindle*
    g. Sting (Police)   7. *Roadie*

16. Which British singer served a stint as house pianist for the Portsmouth Playboy Club?

17. What was the first new wave single to reach the Number One position in the American charts?

18. Which British guitarist started a publishing company called Riot Stories?

19. What was the original title for Elvis Costello's *Armed Forces*?

20. Which well-known singer recently published his first book?

ANSWERS

1. The Sex Pistols.

2. Debbie Harry of Blondie.

3. The Clash.

4. Elvis Costello was the leader of the bluegrass group, Flip City, which in the mid-seventies was doing the London club circuit.

5. The Modern Lovers.

6. "Complete Control." It was released as the follow-up single to "Remote Control."

7. Clover, a band from California.

8. Andy Summers of the Police.

9. Chrissie Hynde.

10. Elvis Costello's father, Ross MacManus, was a singer with the Joe Loss Orchestra.

11. "Don't Take No for an Answer." The song is an angry look at the complicated business relationship that existed between Tom Robinson and Ray Davies. Robinson's first band, Cafe Society, was signed to Davies's record label, Konk. When Robinson left the group, Davies was extremely reluctant to release him from his contract. Eventually, after protracted negotiations, their difficulties were resolved.

12. Phil Spector remixed the song "Rock 'n' Roll High School" from the film's soundtrack album.

13. Ian Dury.

14. Mickie Gallagher, who at the present time is keyboard player for Ian Dury and the Blockheads and the Clash, and who, in the early seventies, was a member of Frampton's Camel.

15. a—5, b—1, c—4, d—2, e—6, f—7, g—3.

16. Joe Jackson.

17. "Heart of Glass," by Blondie, went to the Number One position in April, 1979.

18. Paul Weller of the Jam. So far Riot Stories has published two books of poetry.

19. Emotional Fascism.

20. Sting, of the Police. The book is "a fairy story for modern children" entitled Message in a Bottle.

Fade-out

What's In A Name?
Who Said It?
Charts
Odds and Ends

What's In A Name?

How did these groups or performers get their names?
1. The Rolling Stones
2. The Animals
3. The Boomtown Rats
4. Procol Harum
5. The Velvet Underground
6. Led Zeppelin
7. The Doors
8. Poco
9. Abba
10. Talking Heads
11. Ten Years After
12. Pink Floyd
13. Elton John
14. The Beau Brummels
15. Mott the Hoople
16. Lynyrd Skynyrd

17. Alice Cooper

18. Roxy Music

19. Three Dog Night

20. The B-52's

21. King Crimson

22. The Hollies

23. Steppenwolf

24. Soft Machine

25. Country Joe and the Fish

26. The Lovin' Spoonful

27. Chubby Checker

28. Canned Heat

29. Generation X

30. The Searchers

31. Steely Dan

32. The Surfaris

33. The dB's

34. The Blue Caps

35. The Belmonts

36. The Four Seasons

37. UB40

38. The Ramones

39. Uriah Heep

40. Deep Purple

41. Black Sabbath

42. Jojo Gunne

43. The Pretty Things

44. Buffalo Springfield

45. The Doobie Brothers

These are the real names of various performers. What are the names that they have become famous under?

46. Michael Leibowitz

47. Marvin Lee Aday

48. Rudy Martinez

49. Peter Baker

50. Pauline Matthews

51. Henry Deutchendorf, Jr.

52. Malcolm J.M. Creaux

53. Clive Powell

54. David R. Hayward-Jones

55. James Chambers

56. Eric P. Clapp

57. Stephen D. Georgiou

58. Janis Fink

59. Patricia Holt

60. Herbert Khaury

61. Frank Castelluccio

62. Steveland Morris Hardaway

63. Ellen Naomi Cohen

64. Harry R. Webb

65. John Ramistella

66. Hank Wilson

67. William S. Levise, Jr.

68. Domingo Samudio

69. Cheryl S. La Pierre

70. Joachim Krauledat

71. Perry Miller

72. Elias McDaniels

73. Brian Hines

74. Joseph Mellors

75. Frederick Hibberts

76. William Perks

77. Mark Feld

78. John Simon Ritchie

79. Declan Patrick MacManus

80. Marion Elliot

81. Tom Miller

82. Richard Myers

83. Richard Zehringer

84. Freddie Bulsara

85. Vincent Eugene Craddock

86. Chester Arthur Burnett

87. James Jewell Osterburg

88. Willie Borsey

89. McKinley Morganfield

90. Give the names of the rock performers whose nicknames are listed below:
   a. *Keef*
   b. *the General*
   c. *the Boss*
   d. *Pearl*
   e. *Birdman*
   f. *Slowhand*
   g. *the Ox*
   h. *the Thin White Duke*
   i. *the Lizard King*

ANSWERS

1. The Rolling Stones took their name from a blues song by Muddy Waters called "Rolling Stone Blues."

2. The group was originally called the Alan Price Combo and the Kansas City Five, but their unkempt appearance caused them to be rudely referred to as the "animals." So, with an if-you-can't-beat-'em-join-'em attitude, the group changed their name to the Animals.

3. Boomtown Rats was the name of a street gang described in Woody Guthrie's autobiography, Bound For Glory.

4. Procol Harum was the name of a Blue Burmese cat owned by a friend of the band's lyricist, Keith Reid. The name is garbled Latin for "beyond these things."

5. The Velvet Underground took their name from a book of that title about wife-swapping in suburbia.

6. The name Led Zeppelin was concocted by Keith Moon and John Entwistle of the Who. Originally, Moon and Entwistle planned to use the name for the band they were to start upon leaving the Who. However, when this didn't come to pass, Moon passed the name on to Messrs. Plant, Page, Bonham and Jones. Entwistle later said, "When I heard Jimmy [Page] was going to use it, I was a bit pissed off about it but later on, I didn't care that much. After all, they became an institution."

7. Jim Morrison and Ray Manzarek (founding members of the Doors) were profoundly influenced by a book by Aldous Huxley called The Doors of Perception.

8. The name of the band was originally Pogo, but they were sued by Walt Kelly, the originator of a comic strip of the same name, so they changed it to Poco.

9. *The name Abba is a palindrome adopted from the first letters of the musicians' names: Agatha Ulvaeus, Bjorn Ulvaeus, Benny Andersson, and Annifrid Andersson.*

10. *The term "talking heads" is television jargon for a head and shoulder shot; the most common example would be that of a news commentator.*

11. *Devoted fans of Elvis Presley, the members of this band chose this name because the group was formed ten years after Presley's initial appearance in the charts.*

12. *Pink Floyd was derived from the names of two Georgia blues musicians, Pink Anderson and Floyd Council, admired by original Pink Floyd leader, Syd Barrett.*

13. *His real name was Reginald Dwight, but feeling that it lacked zing, he adopted the moniker of Elton John, which he arrived at by combining the names of two musicians with whom he was close, Elton Dean and Long John Baldry.*

14. *Seeing how record stores always arranged records in alphabetical order, the Beau Brummels chose the name that would place them next to the Beatles, hoping this would familiarize rock fans with their group.*

15. *This English group named themselves after a book by Willard Manus titled* Mott the Hoople, *which in turn took its name from Major Hoople, an early comic-strip character.*

16. *Legend has it that this group took their name to revenge themselves upon their high school gym teacher, Leonard Skinerd, who had harrassed some of them on account of their long hair.*

17. *Vincent Furnier, known to millions as Alice Cooper, came upon the name at a seance where a spirit, identifying herself as Alice Cooper, "spoke" to the participants via a Ouija board.*

18. *The name comes from the British Roxy cinema chain.*

19. *This one was inspired by an Australian aborigine custom; on a mildly cold night the members of the tribe would take one of their dogs into their beds for extra warmth, on a colder night they would take two, and on a very cold night, three.*

20. They were not named after the bomber planes, but after the term used to describe the bouffant hairdos worn by band members Kate and Cindy.

21. According to founding member Robert Fripp, "Pete Sinfield [the band's lyricist] was trying to invent a synonym for Beelzebub."

22. The Hollies took their name from Buddy Holly.

23. The original Steppenwolf was the title of a novel by Herman Hesse.

24. The group took their name from the William Burrough's novel, The Soft Machine.

25. Great admirers of Mao Tse-tung, the group was inspired by one of his quotations, "Every fish in the sea is a potential convert," to take on the name Country Mao and The Fish. Eventually, however, it was decided that this was a bit much and the lead singer's name was substituted for the Chinese leader's.

26. The Lovin' Spoonful took their name from the lyrics of "Coffee Blues" by John Hurt.

27. Chubby Checker's name was donated to him by Mrs. Dick Clark, who said, upon seeing him for the first time, "He's cute. He looks like a little Fats Domino. Like a chubby checker."

28. The name was inspired by the blues song, "Canned Heat," by Tommy Johnson.

29. Generation X was the title of an English book about the depraved youth of the sixties.

30. The group named themselves after the 1956 John Ford western, The Searchers.

31. *Steely Dan* was the name of a sexual device featured in William Burroughs's *Naked Lunch*.

32. The name is a contraction of the title of the Beach Boys' song "Surfing Safari."

33. The group took their name from the abbreviation for decibels, which is *db.*

34. The *Blue Caps*, back-up group for Gene Vincent, took their name from the headgear worn by President Eisenhower while golfing.

35. *Belmont Avenue*, in New York City's Bronx, was the source for the Belmonts (of Dion and the Belmonts fame).

36. *Four Seasons* was the name of a bowling alley where the group performed.

37. *UB40* is the code name of the British unemployment form.

38. The *Ramones* derived their name from Paul McCartney's pseudonym, Paul Ramon (*Ram On*).

39. This English group named themselves after the character in Charles Dickens's novel, *David Copperfield*.

40. "*Deep Purple*" was the name of a song that was popular during the 30's.

41. Originally called Earth, the band changed their name to *Black Sabbath* after seeing a Boris Karloff movie with that title.

42. The group took their name from that of a Chuck Berry song.

43. Bo Diddley had a song called "Pretty Thing." The mid-sixties British group made it plural for themselves.

44. According to group member, Richard Furay, "We were living on Fountain Avenue, Los Angeles—and workmen were tearing up the street to do re-surfacing. Well, they were using these big steamrollers to flatten it all out, and they had a name plate on the side . . . just two large words. *Buffalo Springfield*."

45. *Doobie is Californian slang for a joint. After getting high together, the musicians came to the conclusion that they were "doobie brothers."*

46. *Manfred Mann.*

47. *Meat Loaf.*

48. *. ? . (and the Mysterians).*

49. *Ginger Baker.*

50. *Kiki Dee.*

51. *John Denver.*

52. *Dr. John.*

53. *Georgie Fame.*

54. *David Bowie.*

55. *Jimmy Cliff.*

56. *Eric Clapton.*

57. *Cat Stevens.*

58. *Janis Ian.*

59. *Patti LaBelle.*

60. *Tiny Tim.*

61. *Frankie Valli.*

62. *Stevie Wonder.*

63. *Cass Elliott.*

64. *Cliff Richard.*

65. *Johnny Rivers.*

66. *Leon Russell.*

67. *Mitch Ryder.*

68. *Sam the Sham (and the Pharaohs).*

69. Cher.

70. John Kay.

71. Jesse Colin Young.

72. Bo Diddley.

73. Denny Laine.

74. Joe Strummer.

75. Toots (and the Maytals).

76. Bill Wyman.

77. Marc Bolan.

78. Sid Vicious.

79. Elvis Costello.

80. Poly Styrene.

81. Tom Verlaine.

82. Richard Hell.

83. Rick Derringer.

84. Freddie Mercury.

85. Gene Vincent.

86. Howlin' Wolf.

87. Iggy Pop.

88. Willie DeVille.

89. Muddy Waters.

90. a. Keith Richards (Rolling Stones) b. Jerry Dammers (the Specials) c. Bruce Springsteen d. Janis Joplin e. Peter Townshend (the Who) f. Eric Clapton g. John Entwistle (the Who) h. David Bowie i. Jim Morrison.

Who Said It?

Identify the people who made the following statements:

1. "Rock 'n' roll is phony and false, and sung, written and played for the most part by cretinous goons."

2. "Would the people in the cheaper seats clap your hands? And the rest of you, if you'd just rattle your jewelry . . ."

3. "We've always thought there was more to playing rock 'n' roll than playing 'Johnny B. Goode.' "

4. "I know this won't last. I give it another two years."

5. "We stand for pop art clothes, pop art music and pop art behaviour. We don't change off-stage—we live pop art."

6. "I always stand by Young Communist principles. If I was in Russia in some harsh five-year plan—if it was for the good of the country—I wouldn't mind. I would get joy out of seeing something being done, like new libraries being built."

7. "My first move was to get a Rolling Stone as a boyfriend. I slept with three and then I decided the lead singer was the best bet."

8. "Sorry 'bout the sweat, honey, that's just holy water."

9. "I think there should be a national carnival, much the same as the Mardi Gras in Rio. There should be a week of national hilarity . . ."

10. "The Beatles are the Divine Messiahs. The wisest, holiest, most effective avatars (Divine Incarnate, God Agents) that the human race has yet produced . . ."

11. "All my records are comedy records."

12. "When I first knew Elvis he had a million dollars worth of talent. Now he has a million dollars."

13. "They're always saying I'm a capitalistic pig. I suppose I am. But . . . it's good for my drumming."

14. "I promise you they'll never be back on the show. Frankly, I didn't see the group until the day before the broadcast. They were recommended by my scouts in England. I was shocked when I saw them. It took me seventeen years to build this show, I'm not going to have it destroyed in a matter of weeks."

15. "The only difference between 'boring' and 'laid back' is one million dollars."

16. "I'm not kidding myself. My voice alone is just an ordinary voice. What people come to see is how I use it. If I stand still while I'm singing, I'm dead, man. I might as well go back to driving a truck."

17. "The stage is our bed and the audience is our broad. We're not entertaining, we're making love."

18. "After all, I am the last white nigger."

19. "If people want to make war, they should make a color

war, and paint each other's cities up in the night in pinks and greens."

20. "The Beatles are a plot by the ruling classes to distract youngsters from politics and bitter pondering over disgraced and shattered hopes."

21. "Psycho-politicians are using the Beatle music . . . to hypnotize American youth and prepare them for future submission to subversive control . . . a systematic plan geared to making a generation of American youth mentally ill and emotionally unstable."

22. "Our real followers have moved on with us and are questioning some of the basic immoralities which are tolerated in present day society—the war in Vietnam, persecution of homosexuals, illegality of abortion and of drug taking. All these things are immoral. We are making our own statement—others are making more intellectual ones."

23. "Sometimes I look at my face and I think it looks pretty run down, but considering all I have been through, I don't think it looks bad at all."

24. "Don't interpret me. My songs don't have any meaning. They're just words."

25. "Punk rock? Oh, I've been at it for years, dear."

26. "For the past ten years all I've had to do is stand in the background, sometimes put on a bit of make-up, and look happy to be there."

27. "We're more popular than Jesus now."

28. "I'm changing my image—I'm going to get my teeth

fixed."

29. "We started to do this because we believed in it—not because it was a joke."

30. "I'm a bi-sexual chauvinist pig."

31. "We're not into music. We're into anarchy."

32. "Let's face it: Rock 'n' roll is bigger than all of us."

ANSWERS

1. *Frank Sinatra (1957).*

2. *John Lennon (at the Beatles' Royal Variety performance in 1963).*

3. *Pink Floyd.*

4. *Mick Jagger (1964).*

5. *Peter Townshend (1965).*

6. *Peter Townshend (1966).*

7. *Marianne Faithfull.*

8. *Little Richard.*

9. *Jim Morrison (1969).*

10. *Timothy Leary.*

11. *Bob Dylan.*

12. *Colonel Parker.*

13. *Keith Moon.*

14. *Ed Sullivan, after the Rolling Stones appeared on his show in 1964.*

15. *Glenn Frey (the Eagles).*

16. *Elvis Presley.*

17. *Marty Balin (Jefferson Airplane).*

18. *Patti Smith.*

19. *Yoko Ono.*

20. Pravda, *the Soviet newspaper.*

21. *Rev. David A. Noebel, of the Christian Crusade.*

22. *Brian Jones (1967).*

23. *Janis Joplin.*

24. *Bob Dylan.*

25. *Mick Jagger.*

26. *Bill Wyman.*

27. *John Lennon.*

28. *Keith Richards.*

29. *Paul Stanley (Kiss).*

30. *Lou Reed.*

31. *Sex Pistols.*

32. *Alan Freed (1958).*

Charts

1. What was the first LP to top *Billboard's* charts within two weeks of release?

2. What song held the Number One position for the longest time in the 1960's?

3. What song held the Number One position for the longest time in the 1970's?

4. Which recording artist or group has had the most Number One hits?

5. Which recording artist or group has had the most Top Ten singles?

6. Which recording artist or group has had the most Top Forty singles?

7. Which recording artist or group has had the most singles in the charts?

8. Which recording artist or group has had singles appear in the charts over the longest span of time?

9. Which single remained in the American charts for the longest time?

10. Who are the five most successful songwriters, according to the number of hit records they've had on *Billboard's* Hot Hundred singles charts?

11. Who are the top five producers according to the number of hit records they've produced?

12. What rock LP remained in the charts longer than any other?

ANSWERS

1. The Beatles' Second Album, *released in 1964.*

2. *"Hey Jude," by the Beatles, which remained at the Number One position for nine weeks in the fall of 1968.*

3. *"You Light Up My Life," by Debby Boone, which stayed up at Number One for ten weeks in the fall of 1977.*

4. *The Beatles, who had twenty Number One hits in the* Billboard *Hot Hundred chart.*

5. *Elvis Presley. During his long career Presley had thirty entries in the Top Ten of the* Billboard *Hot Hundred chart.*

6. *Elvis Presley, who had 104 Top Forty hits.*

7. *Elvis Presley. 147 of Presley's singles appeared in the* Billboard *Hot Hundred chart.*

8. *Elvis Presley, who had hit records in the charts from 1956 to 1977.*

9. *"Rock Around the Clock" by Bill Haley and His Comets, which remained in the charts for 43 weeks in 1955.*

10. *Paul McCartney (52), John Lennon (42), Eddie Holland (33), Lamont Dozier (32), and Brian Holland (31).*

11. *Brian Holland (27), Lamont Dozier (26), Bob Crewe (23), Norman Whitfield (21), Lou Adler (20).*

12. *Pink Floyd's* Dark Side of the Moon *(1973) is still in the* Billboard *charts (as of this writing) after over 350 weeks.*

Odds and Ends

1. What was the first rock bootleg to gain wide circulation?

2. What was the longest album title?

3. What was the first rock song to fill an entire side of an album?

4. A special recording featuring music drawn from the earth's great cultural traditions, compiled by Carl Sagan's NASA Voyager Record Committee for the listening pleasure of extraterrestrials, was placed on board a Voyager spacecraft launched in 1977. What piece was selected to represent rock 'n' roll?

5. What was the longest name for a rock group?

6. What was the longest title for a single?

7. What was the first double album of new material ever released by a major rock artist?

8. What six rock 'n' roll groups or performers have had the dubious honor of being featured in their own bubblegum-card series?

9. What was the longest hit single?

10. Match the groups or musicians to the movies they scored.

a. Brian Eno	1. Green Ice
b. Isaac Hayes	2. Friends
c. The Kinks	3. You're A Big Boy Now
d. Elton John	4. Poor Cow
e. Alan Price	5. Sebastion
f. Lovin' Spoonful	6. Shaft
g. Carl Perkins	7. Percy
h. Donovan	8. O' Lucky Man
i. Bill Wyman	9. Little Fauss and Big Halsey

11. What song title has been used the most often for hit songs?

12. What one song has been a hit the most often for different artists?

13. Who are the thirteen rock, soul or folk artists or groups to have had their picture on the cover of *Time* magazine?

14. Match the groups or artists to the record label that they started:

a. The Beach Boys	1. Palladium
b. George Harrison	2. Suede
c. Jefferson Airplane	3. Two-Tone
d. Ray Davies	4. Brother
e. Leon Russell	5. Grunt
f. Elton John	6. New Hormones
g. Moody Blues	7. Dark Horse
h. Bob Seger	8. Go-Feet
i. Jerry Dammers	9. Konk
j. The (English) Beat	10. Shelter
k. Carl Perkins	11. Rocket
l. Howard Devoto	12. Threshold

15. Match the performers to the books they wrote:

a. *The Lords and the New Creatures*

b. *Babel*

c. *Tarantula*

d. *Notes from a Broad*

e. *Warlock of Love*

f. *The Diary of a Rock Star*

g. *Day Break*

h. *I, Me, Mine*

i. *Home Thoughts from Abroad.*

1. *Patti Smith*

2. *George Harrison*

3. *Bette Midler*

4. *Joan Baez*

5. *Robin Williamson (Incredible String Band)*

6. *Jim Morrison*

7. *Bob Dylan*

8. *Marc Bolan*

9. *Ian Hunter (Mott the Hoople)*

16. Which group has lasted for the longest time without any change in its initial line-up?

ANSWERS

1. Great White Wonder, *by Bob Dylan, late 1969.*

2. My People Were Fair and Had Sky in Their Hair But Now They're Content to Wear Stars on Their Brows, *by Tyrannosaurus Rex, released in 1968.*

3. *"Sad-Eyed Lady of the Lowlands," by Bob Dylan.*

4. *"Johnny B. Goode," by Chuck Berry.*

5. *Rock & Roll Dubble Bubble Trading Card Co.*

6. *"Jeremiah Peabody's Polyunsaturated Quick Dissolving Fast Acting Pleasant Tasting Green and Purple Pills" by Ray Stevens, a Top Forty hit in 1961.*

7. Blonde on Blonde, *by Bob Dylan, released in the summer of 1966.*

8. *Elvis Presley, Fabian, the Beatles, the Monkees, the Partridge Family and Kiss.*

9. *The longest hit single was "MacArthur Park" by Richard Harris, which clocks in at 7:20. "Hey Jude," by the Beatles, is second longest at 7:11, with Derek and Dominos' (Eric Clapton's) "Layla" as a close third with a length of 7:10.*
Two Top Forty hits, "Hurricane," by Bob Dylan and "American Pie," by Don McLean, were both over eight minutes long, but were divided in half on the single. Since Top Forty radio stations tended to play only the first side of the singles, these songs can't really qualify for the longest hit song.

10. *a—5, b—6, c—7, d—2, e—8, f—3, g—9, h—4, i—1.*

11. *"Happy." Sunshine Company, the Rolling Stones, Eddie*

Kendricks, Bobby Darin, Nancy Sinatra, Paul Anka, and Hog Heaven have all had hits with different songs entitled "Happy."

12. "Mack the Knife" was a hit for eight different artists within 1956–1960: Les Paul, Billy Vaughn, Richard Hayman and Jan August, Lawrence Welk, Dick Hyman Trio, Louis Armstrong, Bobby Darin, and Ella Fitzgerald.

13. Joan Baez (1962), the Beatles (1967), Aretha Franklin (1968), The Band (1970), James Taylor (1971), Joni Mitchell (1974), Bruce Springsteen (1975), Cher (1975), Elton John (1975), Paul McCartney (1976), Linda Ronstadt (1977), the Who (1979) and John Lennon (1980).

14. a—4, b—7, c—5, d—9, e—10, f—11, g—12, h—1, i—3, j—8, k—2, l—6.

15. a—6, b—1, c—7, d—3, e—8, f—9, g—4, h—2, i—5.

16. The Four Tops. Formed in 1954, they have retained their original line-up to this day. However, it could be argued that the Four Tops are a soul group, as opposed to a rock group, in which case the honors would go to the Who. Formed in late 1963, this English band had no change in its line-up until the untimely death of drummer Keith Moon in 1978.

Index